Original title:
The Tide's Call

Copyright © 2025 Creative Arts Management OÜ
All rights reserved.

Author: Helena Marchant
ISBN HARDBACK: 978-1-80587-409-6
ISBN PAPERBACK: 978-1-80587-879-7

Driftwood Dreams

On the shore where driftwood lies,
A seagull steals my fries.
With a squawk, he takes a dive,
I swear that bird's come alive!

My flip-flops left, they float away,
A crab just laughs at my dismay.
Oh, how I chase, well, sort of run,
While beach balls bounce and have their fun!

The sunburned folks play leapfrog fast,
While one poor chap just fell at last.
The lifeguard tries to look so cool,
But trips and splashes in the pool!

As evening lands with sunset's glow,
We gather round, the laughter flows.
With driftwood dreams beneath our feet,
The beach is where we find our beat.

Shell-Made Wishes

In the sand, I build a throne,
Out of shells and stuff I've grown.
A wishing well, it gleams so bright,
Though jellyfish give quite a fright!

Someone found a fishy hat,
I laughed so hard, my tummy sat.
A hermit crab moves in my boot,
I swear he thinks it's quite the loot!

With seashells stacked, a castle grand,
The king appears—a tiny hand.
But when the waves come rolling in,
My fortress crumbles, oh, such din!

Yet in this place of ocean sighs,
Every day brings a new surprise.
With each shell made and laugh that's shared,
Our seaside tales are never spared.

A Sailor's Soliloquy Beneath the Stars

Oh, captain, where's my sea legs gone?
The fish are teasing, singing a song.
With wobbly toes on deck, I sway,
While gulls chuckle, saying, 'No way!'

My compass points to the fridge, it's true,
For snacks I seek on this wild blue.
Starfish gossip as they flip and roll,
As I trip on waves, losing control.

Urge of the Glistening Waters

A splash, a laugh, a slippery slide,
The ocean's mood is a wacky ride.
Crabs do the conga, shells in the groove,
I join the dance—oh, look at me move!

The bubbles giggle as they pop and play,
As I try to swim a very odd way.
Dolphins flip, and I just flop,
While seagulls swoop in a dizzy drop.

Secrets in the Dunes

Behind the dunes, what secrets lie?
A picnic basket, and crumbs, oh my!
Sandcastles crumble with a great big blast,
As seagulls conspire, they are quite fast.

The wind whispers tales of nobles in sand,
While I build a fortress that's slightly unplanned.
A bucket, a shovel, both now a mess,
Yet somehow, this chaos feels like success.

Gambols with the Moonlit Coral

Under the moon, the corals prance,
I twirl and twist in a goofy dance.
Octopuses laugh with their eight-a-licious glee,
While I trip over seaweed, oh woe is me!

The starfish cheer, doing their best ballet,
As fish join the fun in a colorful array.
Nature's disco, a sight to behold,
With every splash, my laughter is told.

For a Moment, Time Stood Still

As seagulls squawked with glee,
A crab sidled up to me.
I posed like a fancy king,
He danced, oh what a silly thing.

The sun was shining bright,
A seaweed wig gave quite a fright.
I laughed so hard, I lost my shoe,
The ocean giggled, too.

The Allure of the Brimming Wave

With every wave that splashes high,
A fish jumped up to say 'Oh my!'
It wiggled and it flopped about,
We cheered it on with a silly shout.

The beach ball rolled right past my toes,
Chasing it, I tripped on my clothes.
The waves were laughing, full of cheer,
'Let's have a party! Come join us here!'

Boundless Beauty Beneath the Surface

There's beauty lurking in the sea,
A jellyfish just waved at me.
I waved back with a friendly grin,
But it just floated away, akin.

The sunken treasure claimed its fame,
A rusty boot named 'Old McBlame.'
But all the pirates rolled their eyes,
For they lost it in a game of lies.

Ocean's Heartbeat

The waves all danced, what a thrill,
A dolphin flipped with utmost skill.
'Watch this!' it squeaked, but missed its cue,
And belly-flopped, oh what a view!

Shells whispered secrets in the sand,
A clam popped open with a brand.
It laughed so hard, it dropped its pearl,
Splashed me good in a swirly whirl.

Conversations with the Fisherman's Net

Oh net, you speak in tangled threads,
Your stories caught in fishy beds.
You joke of flounders that got away,
And crabs that danced upon the bay.

With every catch, you hold a tale,
Of slippery fish that made you fail.
Your laughter bubbles on the shore,
As gulls above plot fishing lore.

At dawn you whisper to the waves,
Of sunken boots and fishy braves.
In every knot, a punchline hides,
As ocean's humor gently glides.

So here we lay, with salt and cheer,
Your tales will echo, loud and clear.
So many moments we'll create,
Oh net of mine, it's never late!

Horizon's Embrace at Dusk

The sun dips low with a cheeky grin,
As shadows stretch and giggles begin.
The sky bursts forth in hues so bright,
While dolphins leap in playful flight.

A seagull squawks with a sassy flair,
And flips its wings without a care.
The breeze whispers secrets, oh so bold,
Of adventures that will soon unfold.

With sandy toes and laughter loud,
We share our dreams beneath the cloud.
As night unfolds its cozy hand,
The stars come out to join our band.

With every wave, a joke in tow,
We laugh as the ocean puts on a show.
In twilight's glow, we find our glee,
As the horizon embraces you and me!

The Promise of a Quiet Tide

As waters hum a gentle tune,
The sand bids farewell to the moon.
The shells tell secrets from the shore,
While whispers echo, nevermore.

In silence, humorous fish convene,
Plotting pranks, both sly and keen.
A crab in shades finds lost attire,
As waves applaud with foam and fire.

The promise of peace, a giggly thought,
Where silly boaters twist and knot.
With every swell, a chuckle forms,
In playful dance, the ocean warms.

So come, dear friend, let's take a ride,
On whispers and waves, we'll softly glide.
In this quiet, the laughs reside,
Where the playful sea won't ever hide!

Compass Points in the Sea's Canvas

With compass points, we roam the sea,
Chasing fish who giggle with glee.
The north star winks, a cheeky guide,
As we set sail, no need to hide.

Orcas argue about the best bait,
While sea turtles laugh, 'No time to wait!'
Jellyfish jiggle in the breeze,
A dance party where all feel at ease.

Each wave unfurls a map of fun,
As seabirds chirp, 'The journey's begun!'
So anchor down your worries tight,
And drift with laughter through the night.

Every splash, a canvas of cheer,
As we paint our dreams, bright and clear.
So follow the tide, with giggles in tow,
In the sea's embrace, let the good times flow!

Serenade of the Coral Reef

Bubbles rise with every laugh,
Clownfish dance, they cut in half.
Seaweed sways in silly leaps,
While starfish giggle in their sleeps.

An octopus plays the ukulele,
Singing tunes that are quite silly.
Pufferfish puff, oh what a sight!
Turtles join in, they feel just right.

Jellyfish float with a flair so grand,
Making friends with the mutant sand.
Nemo finds his lost sock, what a find!
In the deep, joy is unconfined.

Crabs in hats march with great pride,
Waving at fish who just won't hide.
Corals blush in vibrant hues,
Underwater jazz fills the blues.

Tracing Footprints in the Sand

Seagulls squawk, they steal some fries,
While kids build castles that touch the skies.
Sand between toes, an itchy spree,
As sandy crabs dance, oh so free!

A dog runs by, drags its owner,
Chasing waves like a frenzied loner.
Footprints vanish, the tide takes them,
Leaving behind a seagull gem.

Warmth of sun with a side of chill,
Caught in a moment, time stands still.
The ocean grins, a cheeky tease,
With each wave, it tickles knees.

Beach balls bounce to a silly beat,
Sandy sandwiches taste quite sweet.
Tracing laughter with each new wave,
Fun in the sun, we all must save.

Journey of the Wandering Foam

Foam on the waves, such a frothy plight,
Riding high, it's quite the sight.
A journey starts with a splish and splash,
Rolling through seaweed, making a dash.

With sea cucumbers sharing a joke,
Making bubbles with every poke.
The foam trips over a sunken chest,
To find treasure with no time to rest.

Jiggly and wiggle, oh what a tale,
It races til it begins to pale.
Meeting fish that dance like pros,
Forming whirlpools with silly shows.

At sunset, it giggles as it's swept away,
Into the night, come what may.
A journey's end is a bubbly cheer,
In the ocean's heart, there's nothing to fear!

Call of the Ocean's Heart

Whales are calling, can you hear?
With belly laughs, they bring good cheer.
Dolphins flip in a lively spree,
Ocean's heart beats, wild and free.

Treasure maps floated on a wave,
A pirate's joke, oh how it misbehaves!
Sandy jokes in the salty breeze,
With each swell, laughter never flees.

Seafoam giggles, a bubbly prank,
Spraying walkers, they're on the flank.
Creatures join in a merry dance,
Who knew the ocean had such romance?

With waves that crash and tickle toes,
It sings a tune that endlessly flows.
Just listen close, it's plain to see,
The ocean's heart beats in glee!

Beneath the Moonlit Waves

Crabs wear hats, it's quite absurd,
Seashells gossip, never blurred.
Starfish tell jokes, the best at sea,
While octopuses moonwalk with glee.

Fish hold parties, they dance and sip,
Jellyfish wiggle, a glowing trip.
Whales do karaoke, hit every note,
While seagulls swoop down, snagging a boat.

Dolphins giggle, flipping with flair,
Turtles roll dice, without a care.
Under the surface, it's quite the blast,
Fin-tastic fun, they're having a blast.

So join the party, dive into play,
Waves keep rolling, come what may.
With laughter echoing, beneath the foam,
The ocean's a circus, a watery home.

Dance of the Rising Current

Waves are rhythm, a jig and jive,
Barnacles strut, so alive!
Fish tune in, to the sea's sweet beat,
Crabs tap dance on their tiny feet.

Currents swirl, a merry whirl,
Nudibranchs twirl, as colors unfurl.
Clownfish giggle, in their own prank,
While starry skies winkle with a wink.

Seagulls join in, flap and flail,
As turtles attempt their dizzying trail.
A shrimp solo, bold and brash,
Making big bubbles, in a splendid splash.

So twirl around, don't miss the fun,
Under the night, the party's begun.
With laughter echoing, no need to stall,
Join the merriment, heed the call!

Secrets of the Shoreline

On the beach, where secrets hide,
Sandy toes are put aside.
Crabs with shades, lounging in sun,
While seashells argue, 'Who's the one?'

Hermit crabs change, their homes in haste,
Snapping seaweed, no time to waste.
Fish in sunglasses, looking so sly,
While pelicans dive, oh my, oh my!

Seagulls gossip, with a caw and squawk,
Building castles, that wash with a rock.
Starfish sneak snacks, dipping with flair,
A salty treat, with salt in the air.

So come to the shore, where laughter blooms,
Where every wave brings secret rooms.
With every splash, stories to tell,
The shoreline's laughter, ring a bell!

Song of the Water's Edge

By the water, where stories sing,
Crabs harmonize, it's a quirky thing.
Oysters roll dice, luck on their side,
While fish swap tales, their gills open wide.

Paddleboats giggle, rocks take a stand,
Sponges throw parties, oh isn't it grand?
The water's a stage, performing in grace,
With seaweed dancers, in their vibrant space.

Shells clatter together, a band on the rise,
Bubble-blowing dolphins, aim for the skies.
Aquatic charades, what fun they bring,
As everyone joins in, the tide's own fling.

So sway to the rhythm, feel the delight,
The water's edge sparkles, a magical sight.
With every splash and wave's gentle caress,
Laughter keeps flowing, it's anyone's guess!

Surrendering to the Sea's Invitation

I saw a crab wearing a hat,
The kind you'd think only I'd have.
He waved his claws, he said, 'What's up?'
I left my plans, just to have a laugh.

The waves kept teasing, rolling in,
Each splash a whisper, 'Come on, play!'
I threw my shoes, said 'I'll dive in!'
Who knew a sock could float away?

The seagulls squawked, pretending to sing,
With fishy breath, they cracked me up.
I laughed and slipped, down with the bling,
The ocean's humor filled my cup.

So here I float, with seaweed hair,
A beach bum's joke, that's what I am.
I surrender to the salty air,
And dance like jelly, oh so glam!

Kisses from the Coastal Breeze

Oh, how the wind went for a kiss,
It tickled my cheeks, oh what a tease!
I swayed and stumbled, made a big fuss,
Told it to chill, 'Just take it with ease!'

The pelicans joined, they took a dive,
'We're coming to get you!' they quacked with glee.
I said, 'No thanks, I'm just here to jive,'
They laughed and arranged a petition for me.

The salty air, it had its charms,
With whispers like secrets, it drew me near.
I spun in circles, and then spread my arms,
The breeze laughed loudly, 'Now this is sheer!'

So with a twirl and a playful shout,
I danced on sands like a goofy bird.
Those kisses from the breeze, without a doubt,
Turned my day into a laugh-filled word!

The Language of Shells and Stars

I found a shell that spoke my name,
It told me secrets, like a gossipy friend.
It said, 'You'll never get seashell fame,'
I said, 'Then let's start a trend!'

We crafted stories of fish in hats,
The octopus played a grand old tune.
The starfish clapped, gave us big pats,
Under the watch of a banana moon.

The conch shell said, 'Let's make some noise,'
While crabs were shaking their tiny tails.
I couldn't stop, I was one of the joys,
In the language of jests carried by gales.

So here we stand, in soft, warm sands,
With shells as our mics, what a grand show!
We chat with the stars, and make big plans,
In a funny language, only we know!

Mists of the Morning Tide

The morning mist, it's rather sly,
It tickles my toes as I frolic past.
It hugs my legs, won't say goodbye,
I trip and stumble, but I'm having a blast.

With foggy sneezes, the sun jumps high,
While gulls overhead, play hide and seek.
I shout, 'Come out, you lazy sky!'
The clouds chuckle, 'You're so unique!'

The waves roll in with a bubbly grin,
They lap at my ankles, say, 'Join the fun!'
I splash around, let the laughter begin,
With each silly slip, I'm never done.

So here's to the mist, and wobbly rides,
To morning mischief by the playful sea.
With joy in my heart, the levity guides,
As I surrender to laughter, just being me!

Whispers of the Ocean's Embrace

The ocean sings a silly song,
It tickles toes that dare to throng.
With every wave that splashes near,
It makes us laugh and sheds a tear.

Seagulls squawk in fitting jest,
They steal our fries, they think it's best.
As crabs do dance upon the sand,
We laugh and cheer as they take a stand.

With shells as hats and laughter loud,
We chase the waves, a giggling crowd.
The salty air, it fills with glee,
For ocean mischief sets us free.

Among the waves, the fun won't end,
We play with fish, we dance, we bend.
In every splash, a joy we find,
As sea and laughter are intertwined.

Moonlit Waves and Silent Shores

The moonbeams dance on ocean's crest,
While crabs hold parties, quite the jest.
They wear our socks with such great flair,
As we pretend we just don't care.

The starfish wave with arms of eight,
Inviting us to join their fate.
We tumble over, laugh and squeal,
A night like this, it's quite the deal.

The waves do chuckle, oh so bold,
As secrets of the ocean unfold.
We make our wishes, shout and play,
By moonlit paths, we drift away.

An octopus serves drinks with style,
We toast to fun, and stay awhile.
With giggles bright beneath the night,
Our hearts grow light, our spirits take flight.

Echoes of the Deep

Beneath the waves, the dolphins grin,
With silly flips, they beckon in.
They mock our dances on the shore,
And we respond by laughing more.

The fish don hats and shades of blue,
They party hard, while we pursue.
They swim in circles, just a game,
While giggles echo, who's to blame?

In coral reefs, the colors pop,
The seaweed sways, we just can't stop.
As laughter bubbles through the sea,
We find our joy, we feel so free.

In ocean depths, we lose all time,
With playful waves, we write our rhyme.
The echoes call, and so we heed,
To join the fun, it's all we need.

The Pull of Celestial Waters

The stars above begin to wink,
As fish in gowns begin to sink.
They dance about with flair and style,
Our laughter makes the ocean smile.

The squid serves drinks in shells of gold,
While sea turtles join with tales retold.
They spin and twirl, it's quite the sight,
In waters deep, we find delight.

With every splash, a giggle flies,
The surf supports our wildest tries.
The moon looks down with cheerful beams,
We swim in silliness, fulfilling dreams.

As tides do pull in merry jest,
We ride the waves, we feel so blessed.
In watery realms, where giggles swirl,
The ocean's charm, a joyful whirl.

The Enchantment of the Ocean's Caress

The seagulls squawk with glee,
As waves play tag with the shore,
I try to dance, but I trip,
And get splashed from my knees to my core.

A crab waves its claw, in jest,
As I wiggle in the sand,
A beach ball bounces past my head,
From an overzealous hand.

The sun's too bright, I squint and grin,
Sipping lemonade so sweet,
Turns out it's saltwater, oh dear!
Next time, I'll bring a seat!

With flip-flops flying everywhere,
The children chase their dreams,
While I chase down my runaway hat,
In this seaside comic scene.

Flight of the Sailor's Dream

A sailor dreams of skies so blue,
With fishes wearing hats and ties,
But then he spills his fishy stew,
And finds it's not a big surprise.

His boat is heaving, rocking too,
While seagulls dive and swoop,
I wonder if they're in on it,
A feathered, fishy troop.

He shouts, "Ahoy!" to passing whales,
Who snicker with a splashy grin,
They've seen his ropes and tangled sails,
And know he's bound to spin!

As wind catches the sails just right,
He steers with all his might,
But ends up circling back around,
To hug the shore—what a sight!

Secrets Buried Beneath the Surface

Beneath the waves, a secret waits,
A treasure chest, so bold and grand,
But it's filled with socks, not gold, oh fate!
Guess this is not the pirate's land.

The fish giggle, swim away,
As I search for something neat,
A rubber duck, the prize of day,
For centuries lost to defeat.

Clams gossip in their sleepy shells,
As bubbles burst with playful cheer,
I ask them where their mystery dwells,
They shrug, it's just a watery sphere!

I'll bring my finds to shore one day,
A sock, a duck, a lonely shoe,
And tell the tale as fish parade,
Of secrets deep, absurd but true!

Chasing the Horizon's Glow

I chase the sunset on a board,
With hopes high like a kite,
But it flips me over, oh good lord!
Water's chilly—what a fright.

The fish swim by with a smirk,
As I flounder like a seal,
They know my balance is no perk,
My board's a slippery wheel.

The horizon giggles in the dusk,
As I paddle with all my flair,
My hopes of glory turning to rust,
In this ocean-themed affair.

But laughter fills the salty air,
As I finally stand up straight,
The ocean roars a hearty cheer,
And I know I've met my fate!

The Calligraphy of the Currents

I wrote on grains of sandy shore,
The ocean laughed with each wave's roar.
Seagulls swooped, they stole my pen,
While crabs pirouetted, all but zen.

In bottles tossed, my secrets float,
The fish roll by, they seem to gloat.
I scream my verse, they wiggle near,
And read my words through bubbles clear.

With barnacles, my rhymes adorned,
As jellyfish critiqued, I mourned.
The surf gave way to snickers bright,
As whales sang lullabies, what a sight!

So here I stay, my ink a splash,
As dolphins prance, a joyful dash.
Who knew the sea was such a wit?
I'll draft my next line — if I don't quit!

Portraits of a Sunken Past

Ghosts of fish in frames of coral,
Follow me with grins immortal.
A shipwrecked shoe — it wears a frown,
While mermaids giggle, can't drown.

I found an anchor, now it's art,
A crab's fine home, not too far apart.
With clams as brushes, they paint my tale,
Of underwater antics without fail.

The swordfish strikes a dapper pose,
While laughter bubbles as the seaweed grows.
I smile wide, as seashells clap,
The ocean's gallery, a hilarious map.

Dive deeper now, in glee we plunge,
For humor stirs the oceans' grunge.
In briny depths, we dance with glee,
Painting portraits of absurdity!

A Ballet of Water and Wind

The waves twirled, a grand ballet,
With gusts that laughed along the way.
A surfboard spun like a disco ball,
As wind blew kisses, oh what a hall!

Seagulls swooped in for their parts,
Diving low with twisted arts.
The beach folks cheered, with drinks in hand,
As sandcastles joined the dance, so grand!

Oh, the wind, it took a leap,
While dolphins dove in a joyful sweep.
The ocean's arms embraced us all,
In this inky night, we had a ball!

With laughter swirling, we won't stop,
As bubbles burst and we flip-flop.
In this aquatic scheme, we found a groove,
A jolly jig, come join and move!

Journey to the Wind-Tossed Isle

This trip was wild, we set our sail,
But a seagull snatched our lunch — oh, fail!
With winds that swirled in snickers loud,
We lost our hats; what a rowdy crowd.

The isle appeared with cheeky glee,
As coconuts danced, oh so free!
We built a fort of driftwood bright,
But crabs took over, claiming the night.

Grass skirts waving, we jived on sand,
While sea turtles mocked our clumsy stand.
"Come join us!" they called, with shells in hand,
The sun grinned wide, our own command.

So here we laugh on this isle so fun,
With wind-tossed tales, and days begun.
Each day anew, with joy we feign,
In this sandy circus, we'll entertain!

Journey to the Shoreline's Heart

I set out for the sea, so bold,
With snacks packed tight, and tales retold.
The seagulls squawked, they called my name,
As I tripped on sand—oh, what a game!

My flip-flops flew, in a wild ballet,
While crabs all danced, in their own display.
They pinched my toes, I gave a shout,
But they just waved; this is what life's about!

The sun beamed down, quite a prankster there,
Made me think my sunscreen was to share.
I glowed like a lobster, oh what delight,
As beachgoers chuckled, what a funny sight!

I built a grand castle, with towers so high,
But the waves rolled in, a snooty goodbye.
My fortress collapsed, a sandy romance,
Yet I laughed aloud, no need for a chance!

Beneath the Lull of Surging Waves

Underneath the wave's gentle push,
Mermaids giggled in a joyful hush.
With seashells clacked as their silly tunes,
They danced with dolphins beneath the moons.

A fish in a hat yelled, 'What a show!'
'This isn't a party, but an aquarium flow.'
But fishy jokes are hard to tell,
When all they do is laugh and dwell.

The octopus wore socks, a colorful spree,
Said, 'I'm so trendy, come swim with me!'
But squid was still stuck in a netted bind,
Chasing its own tail, just to unwind.

I joined the laughter, what a silly scene,
With crabs in jackets, dressed so pristine.
Surf's up, my friends, let's take a plunge,
In this ocean of giggles, we'll never grunge!

Dreams Carried by the Currents

Drifting on dreams, I took a ride,
On a rubber duck, all puffy and wide.
The fish shimmied in a conga line,
While I sipped lemonade, feeling divine.

Seashells whispered secrets of the deep,
While seaweed tickled, made me squeak and leap.
Caught in a whirl, who knew it would be,
A water ballet, awkward yet free!

Jellyfish wore hats like fancy gents,
While crabs critiqued with their eloquence.
I laughed so hard, I nearly sank low,
In this current of fun, I let my heart flow.

So come join the splash, the giggles won't stop,
With tides so tricky, we'll dive, jump, and hop.
In every wave, a chuckle abounds,
In these dreamy waters, pure joy resounds!

The Siren's Silent Siren

A siren sang, but oh behold,
Her voice was screechy, a tale so bold.
'Come to my rocks!' she beckoned with flair,
But I just laughed, unruffled by air.

Her hair was tangled, like seaweed gone mad,
With starfish clinging, which made her quite glad.
She winked at me, her charm all a mess,
Yet I chuckled loud, 'Your singing's a stress!'

'Just for a snack, will you join my feast?'
With barnacles seated, to say the least.
I grabbed a sandwich, oh what a scene,
A crusty old fish just wanted to glean!

So on the shore, I found my sweet bliss,
With mermaids laughing in a watery kiss.
The sirens might sing, but I won't be sold—
For laughter's the treasure, more precious than gold!

Voices of the Distant Abyss

In the depths where fish do jest,
A squid once wore a pirate's vest.
He danced with crabs, oh what a sight,
While dolphins laughed at his delight.

A clam complained, he lost his pearl,
While seaweed swayed and gave a twirl.
The jellyfish, with all its flair,
Said, "Do a jig, but don't you care!"

An octopus with juggling kits,
Threw sea cucumbers, make no bits.
The voices echoed through the brine,
As laughter bubbled like sweet wine.

So heed the tales from oceans wide,
Where giggles dance in frothy tide.
A world of whims beneath the spray,
When creatures jest, who needs ballet?

Traces Left by Wandering Seas

Footprints found on sandy shores,
Made by crabs and playful boars.
A seagull swooped, a snack it sought,
While otters giggled, all they caught.

As waves rolled in, the shells conspired,
"Let's hide!" they said, as if they'd tired.
The starfish grinned, planning a coup,
Sailing on flotsam, what a crew!

A fish in shades, so bright and bold,
Flaunted tales from waters cold.
With bubble-beard, he'd surely claim,
To have once swum with Poseidon's fame.

So linger long on shores of cheer,
Where whimsy reigns and joys are clear.
From every splash, a story weaves,
In merry tracks the ocean leaves.

Whispers of the Ocean's Embrace

Beneath the waves where shrimps exchange,
Gossip lightly, not too strange.
"A fish wore socks!" a hermit said,
While seahorses flipped on their head.

The starfish told the funniest joke,
About a whale who loves to smoke.
"Just seaweed, though! It's all so neat!"
As laughter rippled in the heat.

A crab in shades, so diva-like,
Ordered shrimp cocktails on a bike.
The octopus served with a grin,
"Who wants to dance? Now let's begin!"

Amidst the waves of giggly mirth,
Where every splash brings forth new birth,
The whispers swirl in salty foam,
Making the ocean feel like home.

Echoes of the Salty Breeze

In salty air where humor floats,
Fish play pranks and tell odd quotes.
A blowfish puffed, thought he was slick,
While barnacles joined in for a kick.

The waves, they chuckled, full of glee,
As dolphins flipped, oh can't you see?
They surfed on currents, quick and bright,
Turning the ocean into a flight.

A lobster in shades held a grand show,
Critiqued by crabs, they all said, "Whoa!"
With every pinch and every clap,
Echoes rang, like an ocean's tap.

So wander near the briny foam,
Where laughter sings and spirits roam.
Let echoes dance upon your ear,
For in the sea, there's nothing to fear.

Explorations of the Azure Depths

A fish in a bowler hat, quite absurd,
Swims past a crab who's just heard a word.
"Sardines on Sunday!" the clam starts to shout,
As jellyfish laugh and do a little pout.

Sunken ships dance in the turquoise spree,
While snail's telling tales of the wild, wavy sea.
A sea turtle winks, wearing shades and a grin,
"Let's ride the waves, let the fun times begin!"

The octopus plays a game of charades,
While seahorses gossip in elegant parades.
Every flick of a fin, a wacky delight,
In the glorious ocean, where everything's bright!

So grab your flippers and join in today,
With laughter and bubbles, we'll splash and sway.
As every creature here, both big and small,
Is dancing and singing to the sea's funny call.

Tranquility in the Rolling Surf

Sandcastles lean with a lazy sly grin,
While waves tickle toes and begin to spin.
A starfish recites a most silly old rhyme,
That makes crabs do a dance, oh what a fun time!

Seagulls compete for the best silly pose,
One lands on a child wearing sunscreen on nose.
The tide whispers secrets, both joyful and sweet,
As children giggle and chase after their feet.

The beach ball goes flying, a game of mayhem,
While jellys and starfish cheer on like a gem.
With shouts of delight, the laughter does swell,
In this rolling surf, we are under its spell!

A crab in a headband waves back in delight,
He has dance moves to show, all day and all night.
As the sun dips low, and the day turns to night,
We'll cherish the fun, and the waves that feel right!

With Every Incoming Breath

With every wave that tumbles ashore,
Comes a giggle or snicker, never a bore.
Clams wear fine hats, shells glimmer and gleam,
As a dolphin now juggles a bright, fishy dream.

A pineapple floats past, it's just so absurd,
While coral formations whisper every word.
In this world of silliness, joy knows no end,
For every sea creature is here as a friend.

Anemones dance with a wobble and sway,
To the rhythm of bubbles, they party all day.
Each splash tells a story, full of playful cheer,
While a wise old turtle offers some beer.

And when we dive deep, the giggles grow bold,
For who knew the ocean could ever be so gold?
So next time you hear, the ocean's sweet breath,
Remember the joy, and it's life, not death!

The Sand's Silent Secrets

The sand whispers loudly, or is it my ears?
Pirate jokes carried from the moon through the years.
Footprints in giggles, they lead to a barrel,
Of laughter and seaweed, too slippery to handle!

A crab in a blazer talks stocks with a fish,
"They're on the rise, but the tides take a swish!"
With laughter erupting like waves on the shore,
Each grain holds a secret, who could ask for more?

Children dig deep as they search for a prize,
A treasure chest hidden under sunlit skies.
But all they find, is a sock—what a tease!
The ocean's just chuckling, with each gentle breeze.

So if you encounter a shell with a grin,
Join the wave of laughter, let the fun begin.
For every soft whisper beneath sandy spells,
Are the secrets of joy that each moment compels!

Embracing the Rising Swells

Waves come crashing, oh what a sight,
Seagulls squawking with all their might.
I slipped on seaweed, took a dive,
Now my laughter's how I survive.

Shells are hiding, playing a game,
They giggle as I call their name.
The sun is shining, painting the sand,
While wind does tricks, oh isn't it grand?

Buckets of sand, castles we build,
With moats filled with water, dreams fulfilled.
A crab waves hello, my new best friend,
Together we dance, a joy that won't end.

Flip-flops fly off as I run for a splash,
The beach is a stage, oh what a bash!
With every rise, a giggle, a cheer,
Embracing the waves, full of good cheer.

The Rhythm of Restless Waters

The ocean's got moves, a wobbly beat,
It tickles my toes, oh what a treat!
In the surf, I stumble, trip, and fall,
But laughter erupts; it conquers all.

Each wave that charges, a cheeky grin,
Sprays me with water, where do I begin?
The fish are swimming in a silly parade,
I join in the frolic, no need to be afraid.

A dolphin jumps in, does a mid-air spin,
Splashing my hat, oh, what a win!
With each ebb and flow, the jokes galore,
The ocean's a jester, forever I'll adore.

My sandy pants are quite the sight,
Covered in grains, I'm a funny fright.
But oh, the rhythm, it sings to my soul,
In the dance of the waters, I'm always whole.

Lessons from the Weathered Shore

Stones whisper secrets from long ago,
They chuckle and giggle, putting on a show.
The driftwood drifts in a wobbly line,
I listen closely, for wisdom divine.

Seashells gather, a curious crew,
Sharing tales of the ocean they knew.
A hermit crab scuttles in quite a fuss,
He's housing a shell that's gone quite combust!

When storms do approach, the seagulls dive,
While I stand firm, trying to thrive.
The sand and I share a comical frown,
As we both get whipped by the wind's wild crown.

Funny how each wave, a lesson unfurls,
With laughter and joy, the ocean twirls.
The shore, my teacher, with stories to pour,
In this sandy class, I always want more.

A Canvas of Waves and Solitude

Each wave paints laughter upon my skin,
A quirky shoreline, let the fun begin!
With beach towels sprawled and snacks in hand,
I giggle at seagulls plotting their stand.

A flip of the board, the surfboard spins,
I like to pretend that this is how it begins.
Catching a wave, oh what a sight,
But then comes the tumble, oh what a fright!

The sun waves hello, but so does the sunburn,
In a race with my laughter, I always take turns.
With fishy antics, and dramas so grand,
I strike a pose on the shifting sand.

Each sunset fades, inked in bright hues,
While the ocean tickles my mismatched shoes.
A canvas of moments, where giggles collide,
In the splashes of life, I take it in stride.

A Lullaby for the Deep Waters

Bubbles giggle, fish swim in glee,
A crab does a jig, as sprightly as can be.
Starfish chill, their party begins,
While seaweed dances, it twirls and spins.

Turtles wearing hats, oh what a sight,
They swim in circles, filled with delight.
A seahorse plays chess with a clam,
Both taking turns, what a goofy jam!

Dolphins crack jokes, making waves of fun,
Splashing and laughing, no need to run.
Octopus juggles shells with flair,
But drops them all—oh, what a scare!

So drift away now, under the moon,
In this silly sea, you'll hum a tune.
Close your eyes tight, let laughter flow,
For in these waters, the merriment will grow.

Reflections on the Drifting Sea

Waves toss around like a silly pup,
Surfboards dance, like they're all mixed up.
Seagulls mime, and the winds act coy,
As crabs wear shades, they strut with joy.

The sun does winks, while the clouds play peek,
Fish do impressions, oh, what a freak!
A whale starts singing a high-pitched song,
All the sea creatures hum along, strong.

Sailing ships laugh as they drift with style,
They loop and twirl, making waves all the while.
A clam flips seashells, tries to impress,
But ends up stuck—oh, the ocean's a mess!

So sail with a grin, let your worries go,
Join the sea party, dive deep down below.
In this watery realm, where laughter is free,
Every moment shines bright, just like the sea.

Shadows in the Misty Horizon

In the morning mist, shadows play hide and seek,
A dolphin wears glasses, looking quite chic.
The jellyfish float, with an elegant sway,
While sea cucumbers nap, dreaming of play.

A pirate's ghost, with a friendly grin,
Tries to teach barnacles how to begin.
"Yo-ho-ho! Join me," he slyly will say,
While crabs start a rumor—"He's lost his way!"

The sun sneezes rays that tickle the sea,
A plankton parade, oh what a spree!
Sardines in suits strike poses galore,
As fish munch their snacks, yelling, "We want more!"

So drift through the shadows, let laughter arise,
Put on your best smile, wear your sea disguise.
In this watery world, where weirdness is norm,
The fun never ends—oh, it's quite the charm!

Voices from the Sunlit Depths

In the glow of the sun, the fishes converse,
A clownfish tells tales, but they're all in reverse.
"Did you see the octopus dancing a jig?
He tripped on a starfish—oh, look at him gig!"

The corals are gossiping, secrets galore,
As shrimp play the role of the neighborhood lore.
"Did you hear about Sally, the curious seal?
She tried to learn surfing, but lost her appeal!"

A turtle speaks softly, sharing quiet dreams,
While sea urchins chuckle and form little teams.
"Let's put on a show, dazzle the sun!
With all of our antics, we'll surely have fun!"

So dive down below, where laughter runs fast,
With tales and antics, that surely will last.
In the depths of this world, where stories run wild,
The voices of ocean, forever beguiled.

Chasing the Distant Horizon

With buckets and spades, we set our quest,
Determined to find treasure, we think we're the best.
But all we discover is seaweed delight,
As crabs scuttle past, giving us quite a fright.

We chase down the waves, but they tease and they dash,
Like a choir of giggles, they swirl and they splash.
The seagulls laugh loud, with their raucous refrain,
While we trip on our towels, oh what a grand pain!

We build sandy castles, that don't last a tick,
Then a wave leaps up, like a playful old trick.
There's nothing like laughter when things go awry,
As we shake off our spills and re-watch the sky.

So here on the shore, we each take a seat,
With sand in our hair, it's quite the retreat.
But the stories we share make every mishap right,
In this wacky, warm glow of the sun's fading light.

The Ocean's Lullaby

The ocean hums softly, a tune in the breeze,
While fish play the piano, what a sight to see!
They flounder and flop, oh so out of tune,
With a splash and a giggle, they dance to the moon.

We join in the fun, with our own little song,
Unruly and wild, it can't be that wrong.
A seaweed hat on, we jiggle and sway,
While the crabs in the sand nod along on display.

The jellyfish twirl, in their wonky cha-cha,
While sea turtles bop, like they've just hit the piña.
The waves keep on laughing, as they roll in and out,
It's a concert of folly, without any doubt!

So grab your old friends, let the laughter flow free,
As we dance by the shore, where the salty waves see.
Life's rhythm is funny, it's a wave we can ride,
In this whimsical world of the sea's great tide.

A Symphony of Surf and Stone

The surf plays a tune on the rocky old shore,
With a splash and a crash, who could ask for more?
The gulls add their notes, cawing loud and clear,
As the sand dunes chuckle, oh humorous cheer!

A crab conducts with its pinchers held high,
While the shells make a chorus, they sing with a sigh.
A sea star joins in, with a wiggly flare,
And together they groove, without any care.

The rocks tap their feet, to the beat of the sea,
With the murmur of shells joining in with glee.
Each wave is a stanza, each foam is a note,
As the beach comes alive, on this grand old boat.

So dance, if you can, to this symphonic play,
With laughter and joy, we lose track of the day.
In this concert of chaos, we find our own role,
On this wild, wonderful ride for the soul.

Waters That Bind

The shoreline extends, with treasures to find,
While we gather our gear, our laughter entwined.
With sand on our feet and sunburns galore,
We search for adventure, oh, what's in store?

We try to catch waves, but we just end up splashed,
As the ocean keeps giggling, our plans are outclassed.
A seagull swoops down, steals our lunch in a blink,
Leaving us dumbfounded, we can't help but wink.

The sand's now our seat, as we sit and we jest,
With a crab as a guest, we are truly blessed.
He nods in agreement with each silly joke,
As the sun plays a trick, and the sand's start to soak.

So here's to the fun that our splashes create,
In the waters that bind, we can laugh and relate.
With friendships like seashells, unique in their grind,
We'll dance with the waves, leaving worries behind.

The Hunter and the Hunted

A crab scuttles fast, it slips and it flops,
While I chase it down, oh how my heart hops!
It throws me a wink, and before I can pounce,
It digs in the sand, oh what a sly bounce!

With bucket in hand, I thought I'd be sleek,
But the waves start to laugh, oh how they do speak!
They pull me right in, what a slippery game,
Now I'm the one who has lost all my fame!

The seagulls just caw as they circle above,
They seem to be taunting me, isn't it love?
I slip on a shell, then twirl and I spin,
And next thing I'm shouting, "Hey, where have you been?"

In this comical chase, I'll soon lose my pride,
But laughter's the bait, and I'm along for the ride!
So here's to the battles we all like to wage,
Where sometimes a hunter becomes the main stage!

Revelations at Water's Edge

A hermit crab found a shell so divine,
With a raving review, it said, "This is mine!"
But as it strutted, the shell rolled away,
And now it's just chasing, well, that's how we play!

At the water's edge, I spot a wet dog,
He's digging for treasure, I'm stuck in a fog.
He leaps with excitement, shakes off the sea,
And splashes me good—what a sight for me!

I ponder the wonders when drinking some foam,
When suddenly, out pops a fish in my home!
"Excuse me," it yells, "but you've stepped on my teeth!"
I apologize quickly, trying to find peace!

With laughter and joy at this wacky beach spot,
Each creature reminds me, it's fun we've forgot.
The water keeps calling, we giggle and twirl,
In this sea of confusion, let's give it a whirl!

When Stars Touch the Sea

One night I sat dreaming on warm, sandy shores,
While stars above danced, oh how they do roars!
The moon whispered softly, "Please don't fall in!"
But I tripped on a wave, and it chuckled with glee!

As I floundered and flapped, a fish swam on by,
It winked and it laughed, "Hey, don't be so shy!"
"Join us for a swim, the water's just fine,
But watch for the crabs, they are gobbling up time!"

The waves told me secrets of mermaids and gnomes,
While I tried to chat with a couple of foam.
"Excuse me," I said, "do you all know the score?"
But they bubbled away, leaving me wanting more!

The stars twinkled brightly, with mischief in sight,
As the ocean just giggled, oh what pure delight!
With laughter surrounding, the night couldn't fade,
As I danced with the waves—as if they had played!

Shifting Sands

On the beach, oh so fine, I built my grand fort,
But the wind had a laugh, said, "This is no sport!"
It blew a sweet whisper, and down came my walls,
Now my castle's just memories, it echoes and falls!

Seagulls dive bombing, I cover my fries,
They squawk of their treasures, oh such crafty spies!
With breadcrumbs as bait, they circle and swoop,
While I'm left standing, and feeling the goof!

The sand shifts beneath, just like my own fate,
I slip on a patch, notice my shoes debate!
"Should we sink in the dunes or run off with a crab?"
Oh, life's such a riddle, and I'm not a fab!

But laughter erupts as I roll with the waves,
For each shifting grain holds the stories of brave.
I giggle and stumble, oh what a grand show,
As fun in the sand is the way we should go!

Ancient Echoes

In the echoes of oceans, the whales sing their song,
While the dolphins join in, oh how they belong!
But I try to join in with a splash and a shout,
And instead, they just giggle, oh what's that about?

On an old salty rock, I met a wise crab,
"Where are you headed?" I asked with a jab.
He clicked and he clacked, "Not far from the shore,
Just following fish, and I'll find even more!"

"Hey, don't take my bait!" I yelled to the sea,
But the waves just responded, "Oh, come dance with me!"

With each ancient ripple, I splashed and I spun,
Life's silly surprises are all meant for fun!

So heed all the echoes of laughter and cheer,
Embrace every moment, let go of the fear!
For in these wild waters, where joy is the goal,
We become the true treasures, the heart of the whole!

Lure of the Endless Blue

A crab in a top hat, he dances with glee,
While fish in tuxedos sip tea by the sea.
Jellyfish float by, not a care in their way,
Throw a party, they say, it's a perfect beach day!

Seagulls perform acrobatics, quite mad,
They steal fries from kids, oh, how they are bad!
With sandcastles crumbling, the waves come on by,
And laughter erupts, as the buckets run dry.

The sun plays peek-a-boo, a bright, silly game,
While kids try to catch waves, but all end up lame.
Oh, the sand is just sticky, like gum on a shoe,
Yet joy is infectious in this oceanic view!

So grab your floatie, the fun has begun,
We'll ride the soft waves, oh, this life is a pun!
With sunburns as badges and giggles galore,
We embrace all the chaos, who could ask for more?

Harmony of the Deep

A dolphin does the foxtrot, so quick on his fins,
While turtles debate on who's winning at spins.
They both take a break with a shellfish café,
And argue if krill makes a better soufflé!

An octopus, dressed like a disco-ball star,
Offers dance lessons, he's the best by far.
Fish in the back, they all try to keep time,
But flounders are floundering, it's not sublime!

A clam cracks a joke, it's an old, crusty pun,
And laughter erupts — who knew clams could have fun?
With bubbles and giggles, the seaweed we sway,
Each sway is a memory, gently drifting away.

Oh, the rhythm of bubbles, the joy of deep thrills,
We dance with the current, oh, what funny chills!
In the heart of the ocean, all our cares are so few,
We thrum like the waves, what a jovial crew!

Cradled by the Gentle Swells

A starfish on a hammock is enjoying the breeze,
He waves to his buddies, "Come join me with ease!"
But seahorses squabble, each claiming a spot,
While crabs roll their eyes, think it's all quite fraught.

The pelicans are diving, they're horrible spies,
Flipping sandwiches high, oh, what a surprise!
But fish with their forks, are sipping on juice,
While mermaids chuckle at the chaos profuse!

A whale in a top hat sings sweet serenades,
With dramatic flair, in the cool ocean glades.
But he's eaten a sandwich, now feeling quite slow,
"Next time, I'll just stick to my plankton," he'll crow!

Each swell is a belly laugh, a jig of pure glee,
In this watery world, we always feel free.
So come, take a plunge, let your worries be left,
For joy in the waves is the best kind of gift!

The Rhythm of Distant Shores

A fish with a fedora prepares for a trip,
He's gathering sea-snacks, no chance to skip.
The crabs look confused, think he's lost his mind,
"Who wears hats in the ocean?" they chuckle and grind.

The coral makes comments, it's stylish and bright,
"Your fashion's outdated, but I like the delight!"
A whole school of minnows dance tango and twirl,
Each flick of their tails isn't just a sweet whirl.

The waves clash like cymbals, creating a song,
As jellyfish sway, humming all night long.
Even the starfish join the conga line,
Though they move quite turtle-like, it's still divine!

So gather your friends, let the laughter revive,
In the shores of hilarity, we all come alive!
With every wave crashing, a giggle unfolds,
This ocean of joy, more precious than gold.

Secrets Beneath the Surface

A crab in a tux, dancing with flair,
Jellyfish doing tricks, they float in the air.
Clams holding secrets, they giggle and pout,
While seagulls plot mischief, never in doubt.

A turtle in shades, sunbathing with style,
Fish throwing a party, it'll last for a while.
Sandcastles scheming to guard all the loot,
While starfish play cards with a fish in a suit.

An otter's a lifeguard on patrol with a whistle,
Shells all agree, it's a crazy bristle.
Dolphins in laughter, make waves just for fun,
Under the surface, the jokes have begun.

So dive into antics, embrace all the cheer,
In the deep ocean's laughter, there's nothing to fear.
With secrets afloat, it's a lively parade,
In this whimsical world, let shenanigans cascade.

Dance of the Endless Swell

Waves waltz gracefully, in a shimmery dress,
Clams start to tango, they put on a mess.
A fish leads the way, with a fin raised up high,
While gulls attempt pirouettes, and miss—oh my!

Bubbles burst merrily, popping with glee,
As turtles take selfies, underwater spree.
A starfish in sneakers, can't keep up the beat,
While crabs on the sideline just wiggle their feet.

Seashells wear hats, oh, the fashion is bold,
An octopus DJ spins tunes made of gold.
Dancing together in the swell's wild embrace,
It's a hoot and a half, what a comical place!

So come join the revel, in the surf's playful curl,
With laughter and rhythm, let the fun unfurl.
Each splash a new giggle, each wave a soft sigh,
In the dance of the ocean, let your worries fly!

Where Seafoam Meets Whispering Sand

A seagull in shades struts along the shore,
Sipping on seaweed, it's a feast to adore.
Sandcastles chuckle as the tide creeps near,
Rolling their eyes at the mermaid's last beer.

Crabs play hopscotch on delicate shells,
Whispers of laughter, oh, the stories they tell.
Seashells in circles, gossip with flair,
"Did you see the one wearing a crab on its hair?"

Footprints in sand chasing waves that retreat,
As the fish make a splash, oh what a treat!
Jellybeans bobbing and giggling along,
All join in the laughter, a sweet ocean song.

So listen to secrets that ebb in the night,
Where foam meets the shore in pure, silly delight.
Let nature's own circus be your own joyful brand,
For fun's where the sea meets the soft, whispering sand.

Heartbeats of the Harbor

A harbor's a party, with boats all aglow,
Gulls feasting on fries, stealing the show.
Fishermen grumble, their bait's gone awry,
While a fish tells a joke, and the nets just sigh.

Docks dance in rhythm, swaying to the beat,
As sea lions lounge, they can't find a seat.
A crab with a conch shouts, "It's time for a race!"
While otters play tug-of-war, just for good grace.

Seashells in laughter, wearing caps and bow ties,
Fishing boats flash lights, like stars in the skies.
Every wave that crashes, a heartbeat of cheer,
A harbor alive, with giggles ringing clear.

So put on your laughter, let it echo and sound,
Beneath all the surface, such joy can be found.
For in this grand harbor, where memories twirl,
Each moment a chuckle, each giggle a whirl.

Ebb and Flow of Forgotten Memories

I threw my shoes in the sea,
They danced and swayed so free.
A crab grabbed one and made it his,
Now it's his throne; he's living in bliss.

A fish winked as he passed me by,
With a wink so sly, I'll tell you why.
He whispered tales of old and gray,
Of sailors lost in the milky way.

My bucket's now a fish parade,
With tiny fins and bright arrayed.
They tell me secrets, oh so grand,
Of underwater dreams, not quite planned.

As waves laughed loud, they said to me,
"Next time, bring snacks, we'll feast at sea!"
So I shared some chips, hand over hand,
Turns out fish love a good snack brand!

Tides of Change and Reflection

The ocean's mood swings like a teen,
It giggles and scoffs, oh so mean.
Today it's calm, tomorrow it roars,
It plays peekaboo behind sandy shores.

I built a castle, oh so grand,
But the next wave had other plans at hand.
It laughed so hard, it almost cried,
"Your sand is weak; come join the ride!"

A seagull landed, stealing my fries,
With a cheeky squawk, oh, what a surprise!
We haggled, bartered, exchanged the loot,
He got my fries; I grabbed his suit!

"Come surf with me," said a dolphin spry,
I said, "No thanks, I'd rather stay dry!"
He laughed and splashed, creating a scene,
Now I'm left with this very wet green.

Beneath the Waves' Whisper

There's a clam who thinks he's wise,
He tells the tales beneath the skies.
But when the tide goes up and down,
He just pretends, wears a crown.

The octopus dances, all arms in sway,
While crabs hold a 'crab walk' ballet.
They tell jokes about the fish they've caught,
Trust me, it's the best laugh you've sought.

Anemones wave like our hands at shows,
Swaying like dancers in little bows.
They giggle softly; they're in the zone,
With secrets hidden, never alone.

"Bring cupcakes next time you take a dip!"
Chanted a starfish on my sunken ship.
I promised food, but what came to mind?
A deep-sea feast of the weirdest kind!

Dreamscapes of the Aquatic World

In a bubble dream where fish wear hats,
A puffer fish sings with the talkative chats.
They sip on seaweed smoothies galore,
While dolphins slide through the ocean's floor.

There's a jellyfish jelly, that's all the rage,
Making waves like a cool dance stage.
Sea turtles glide in with style and grace,
Winning all swims in this maritime race.

A crab plays chess with a group of seals,
They bet on fish, making crazy deals.
With every move, the laughter ignites,
A splash of fun under moonlit delights.

But as the currents carry me away,
I'll pack my dreams for another day.
With salty kisses from the sea's sweet breath,
I'll return again for more ocean prep!

Embrace of the Lunar Pull

A crab in my pocket, he squeaks with delight,
He thinks that my shirt is a comfortable site.
The moon in the sky gives a cheeky, wide grin,
As fish try to tango with a jellyfish kin.

The seagulls all gather, they ruffle their feathers,
And argue quite loudly about the best weathers.
With fries in my hand, I run from the chase,
Those feathered bandits have no sense of space!

The beach ball escapes, it's off with a bounce,
A dog makes a leap like he's out for a pounce.
The sandcastle's crown, it's swept by a wave,
We're all just some fools, in the ocean's big cave.

As twilight approaches, we give a loud cheer,
"To all of our troubles, just leave them right here!"
With laughter and splashes, we dance on the shore,
Life's too much of a joke, so let's laugh evermore!

Murmurs in the Surf

The ocean is gossiping, can you hear the sound?
It whispers of treasures buried deep underground.
A clam starts to sing, what a curious tune,
While crabs throw a party beneath the bright moon.

A fish in a tux behaves like a pro,
He waltzes with seaweed, oh what a show!
A dolphin then flips, trying to outdo,
The seagull who dances with moves tried and true.

There's laughter in bubbles, and pranks by the tide,
As starfish play poker, their bets far and wide.
The seaweed crew cheers with a jolly old roar,
For oceanic antics, we always want more!

So join in the fun, bring your best shell hat,
We're dancing with sea creatures—imagine that!
With waves as our beat, we'll shimmy and twirl,
In this playful world of our underwater swirl.

Shades of the Roaming Sea

A fish with a bow tie competes in a race,
While walruses comment with bliss on his pace.
The octopus juggles, his gags never fail,
While turtles flip burgers, oh, what a tale!

In swirls of confusion, the currents all tease,
As snails on surfboards ride high on the breeze.
Anemones giggle, they wave at the show,
While clowns in the coral steal bits from the flow.

Along comes a pirate, half-lost in his map,
He's seeking the gold, but is stuck in a trap!
With seahorses laughing, they point and they jest,
"Your treasure's a donut, you've failed the quest!"

But who needs the gold, with these friends by our side?
We'll sail on the waves, let our laughter be our guide.
With humor so rich, and a splash of delight,
We'll embrace every moment, from morning till night!

Dreams of the Cresting Wave

A wave rolls in yearning for a new friend,
It whispers of mischief, on which we depend.
A floating pineapple joins the parade,
As surfers and seals create quite the charade.

The gulls start a ruckus, they squawk in a line,
With sunglasses on, they sip sea salt brine.
A hermit crab struts in a chocolate chip shell,
While starfish take bets on who'll dance the best swell.

There's laughter that tumbles like foam on the shore,
Each beach day a treasure, with humor galore.
Our footprints in sand, they tell stories of fun,
As the sunsets shine brightly, our antics weigh a ton.

So raise up your drink, made of sand and of sea,
Let's toast to the laughter, as wild as can be!
With dreams of the ocean and smiles all around,
We'll ride every wave till the stars are profound!

Currents of Ancient Memories

Once I tried to walk on waves,
Ended up just making splashes,
The seagulls laughed, oh what a show,
As I danced in salty crashes.

Old crabs peeked from rocky homes,
Waving claws like they know me well,
Shouting tales of lost sea combs,
While I giggled at my own swell.

A fish gave me a sideways glance,
As if to say, 'What's this charade?'
I took a bow, it made my pants,
And off he swam, quite unafraid.

Those memories cling like seaweed strands,
In the ebb and flow, we all play
Life's a joke by ocean's hands,
With laughter rolling every day.

Reflections on the Water's Edge

I saw my face in the sunset glow,
The ocean winked, it's in on the joke,
With every wave, my worries flow,
And a rubber duck watched as I choked.

A crab tried to steal my sandwich bite,
I chased him down, we had a race,
He danced sideways, quite a delight,
While I just blushed at my own pace.

The waves rolled in, a playful tease,
As I flipped my hat, it took a dive,
The shore just laughed, with such ease,
"Your hair's a mess, but you're alive!"

So I tossed my worries to the wind,
Let the tide carry them away,
Life's too short to be all pinned,
I'll bask in laughter every day.

A Song of Salt and Serenity

Salted air and laughing friends,
We made a pact to make a splash,
With water guns and pile-up trends,
In the sun's embrace, we made a crash.

A dolphin peeked, it said, "Come play!"
And we all giggled, hopped, and squealed,
Who knew the waves could require ballet,
With flip-flops on, our fate was sealed.

The seagull swooped, what a fierce dive,
To steal my fries right off my tray,
As we chased him back, how we thrived,
Caught in the giggles of our day.

Every wave a chorus of fun,
With the sun setting, we watched at ease,
The ocean sang for everyone,
As we danced beneath its tease.

Beneath the Blue Horizon

In the morning mist, I took a plunge,
My splash echoed, a watery cheer,
Mermaids showed up for their grunge,
With glitter tails and joyous sneer.

I built a castle, moats and flags,
But the tide saw it and said, "Oh please,"
With a wave it laughed, stole my tags,
As I tried to chase it, made me freeze.

The big blue laughs, we kick and play,
With jellyfish dancing everywhere,
"Go on," they say, "Join the ballet,"
While I twirl and try not to scare.

So here beneath the endless sky,
Where laughter bounces as waves do swell,
I chase the fun, oh me, oh my,
In this shimmery world, all is well.

www.ingramcontent.com/pod-product-compliance
Lightning Source LLC
Chambersburg PA
CBHW060138230426
43661CB00003B/477